How to Monetize a Small Blog

By Luke Weil

Glossary

How To Monetize a Small Blog – Introduction

It was not all that long ago that many of the most successful bloggers founded their sites with no intent other than to create a forum in which they could express themselves and communicate with others who shared a similar interest in a particular subject. Any financial success these bloggers achieved was nothing more than a happy accident -- or so they claimed -- pulling aspiring bloggers into the field with very little in the way of a blueprint for success.

I was one of those aspiring bloggers, and when I started out all I knew was that I wanted to spend my time and energy working on something that provided me with an opportunity for creative expression and allowed me to address subjects I felt were worthy of widespread discussion. I was well aware of the need to generate revenue, but the mindset I adopted was similar to those bloggers who had succeeded before me:

Treat blogging as nothing more than a passion and it will eventually become profitable.

Surely you can see the flaws in that approach, particularly when it comes to the likelihood of founding a popular blog that is reliably profitable and is stable enough that you can make a long-term commitment to ensuring its continued success. It is a strategy that only works for a select few, as it requires not just skill, creativity and perseverance, but also a healthy dose of sheer luck to survive long enough that profitability just *happens*.

When I look back at how I ended up where I am today, I often wish that there was some way to go back in time to tell the Luke Weil of so many years ago about all that I have learned since I founded that first blog. There is not a single thing that I would do the same if I were able to do it all over again, which is why I feel it is so important to share the information I have learned over the years so that you do not have to endure some of the unnecessary difficulties I had to overcome while creating a number of profitable blogs.

The very first mistake I made was failing to create a profitability model right from the start. As I mentioned, I was under the impression that thinking about potential sources of revenue was a fairly low priority, so I focused solely on writing about what I felt were critically important subjects with no goal other than to provide information and to offer my own personal analysis. While focusing on the quality of the content is obviously essential when it comes to long-term success in blogging, it is still impossible to consistently create high-level content without any means of financial support.

It is for this reason that this book is centered on the strategies I have found to be effective in generating revenue for blogs in a way that does not distract from the quality of the content. To ensure long-term blogging success and security, monetization strategies have to be considered in the blog's early stages so the structure and content can be developed in concert with one another. This ensures that the blog functions well right from the start and that visitors to your site are able to become familiar with the layout without having to adapt to the constant changes you would have to make to accommodate new profitability strategies.

Perhaps you are resistant to the idea that a blog has to have profitability as one of its primary goals. After all, there was a point in which I felt that way too. It seemed -- at the time, at least -- almost unfair to devote my efforts to anything other than the content I was providing to my readers, and there were times in which I felt that using monetization strategies would make my readers feel like they were being used somehow. Obviously, that could not be further from the truth.

Monetization strategies are key to your survival as a blogger, and the appropriate use of these strategies ensures that your readers are able to have continued access to the valuable content you provide. Once I reached the point in which I could no longer afford to run my blog without a source of revenue to support it, I realized that monetization strategies are absolutely necessary and represent the main reason that online readers are able to have access to such a vast informational resource.

You don't have make it a goal to increase your profit margin by a certain percent each quarter, but you do have to make profitability and revenue generation a key component of your blogging strategy. There are certainly bloggers out there whose main focus is to make a lot of money from their blogs and are able to succeed in doing so, but they also understand that they have to be providing something of clear value to have any sort of success. It is my belief that a balanced approach that focuses equally on the quality of the content and on the quality of the monetization strategy represents the clearest path to success.

In this book, however, the strict focus will be on specific monetization strategies that you can apply to your blog regardless of the blog's subject or genre. Each chapter covers a different strategy, with specific advice and examples for getting the most out of each while also ensuring that your readers are not distracted or put off by their use. These strategies include:

- Direct advertising
- Sponsored content
- Display advertising
- Advertising networks
- Affiliate marketing
- Branded sponsored campaigns
- Mailing lists

As you can see, some of these are direct monetization strategies, while others generate revenue indirectly by promoting your brand to a wider audience. Each chapter will aim to demonstrate the many different ways in which these strategies can be applied to your blog while also explaining how revenue is generated through the use of each.

You do not have to apply every strategy to your blog, but a varied approach to monetization is much more likely to yield positive results. With a solid revenue strategy in place, you can ensure that you are able to continue to reliably provide vital information to your audience while simultaneously working toward achieving a comfortable level of financial security.

Direct Advertising - People Contact You!

Advertising is the most common strategy used by bloggers looking to monetize their site, and readers have come to expect this sort of approach whenever they visit any site whether it is large or small. While nearly every site includes some form of advertising strategy, a significant portion make critical errors that affect the strength of their readership and reduce the potential advertising revenue they generate. In the chapters that follow we will discuss several different forms of advertising, but this chapter will specifically focus on direct advertising sales.

Direct advertising is an excellent strategy under the right circumstances, but there are instances in which its use can have unintended consequences. It is important to consider your specific audience demographics in order to determine whether or not direct advertising is an appropriate strategy for your blog, as the size of your audience, their common interests and their loyalty to the blog all play a role in the success or failure of a direct advertising strategy.

The potential impact on the user experience must also be weighed against the potential revenue a direct advertising campaign will generate, as it should be obvious that it does not make much sense to engage in a strategy with risks that outweigh the rewards. Understanding how to evaluate the risk versus the reward is just as important as understanding how to implement direct advertising, so this chapter will address both of these essential issues in detail so that you are armed with all the information you need to be successful.

Determine When Direct Advertising Is Appropriate

The potential revenue generated by direct advertising is fairly limited when compared to other strategies such as the sale of digital products, and this is due to the fact that there is only so much space on a site that can be sold to an advertiser before it begins to have an adverse effect on the reader. There are two main types of direct advertising, and it is quite likely that you have seen both in action:

• Text links
• Banner and sidebar ads

Text links can be included within blog posts or on the site itself, and in many cases bloggers try to make these links appear as organic as possible. Sponsored content could fall under this category, but there is so much to discuss regarding this strategy that it will have to wait for a later chapter. As for banner ads, these are the ads that can occupy a wide variety of places on the site, but many blogs make the mistake of overloading their site with so many ads that users are completely distracted and do not bother to return.

Since there are some risks associated with direct advertising, it is important that the potential revenue generated by the advertising is worth the risk. Advertisers pay according to the size of the audience they reach, so a blog has to have a fairly large readership to really make direct advertising worthwhile. How much an advertiser is willing to pay for space on your blog will also depend on how relevant your subject is to what it is they are advertising. A niche website that attracts consumers who are very likely to be interested in a company's product or service will yield far more advertising revenue per visitor than a site with a larger audience whose interests tend to be much more diverse.

Know Your Audience

If your audience is large enough to warrant a direct advertising strategy, you have to first make sure you have a deep understanding of the makeup of your audience. This does not mean that you should make an effort to get to know your audience on a personal level by being active in the comments section (although there are other reasons why you should engage your audience in this way), but rather that you have to know their specific demographics so you can effectively market your audience to potential advertisers. If you cannot show why an advertiser would specifically benefit from buying space on your blog, why would they?

To appropriately market your audience, you have to delve into your site analytics to collect the specific information that will appeal to potential advertisers. This would include the basic information available in an analytics program (age, location, interests, etc.) along with data detailing the level of audience interaction typical on your site (total time on the site, level of engagement, returning visitor rate, etc.).

If you want to get a more well-rounded view of your audience, surveys are a great option. You may have to provide some sort of incentive to get your audience to participate, but in most cases a simple and brief survey will get a decent return rate. Any time you can provide a great deal of information about your audience, the likelihood of generating direct sales revenue increases at an exponential rate.

Attract Advertisers Using a Passive Approach

Seeking out potential advertisers can be one of the most frustrating and time-consuming tasks for a blogger, so don't bother doing it. Instead, let advertisers come to you by including a link on your site that is easily located and provides specific details and contact information for parties interested in buying advertising. A site that has enough visitors to warrant using direct advertising strategies will get plenty of interested parties without having to actively seek them out, and passive ad sales are far less time-consuming and much more worthwhile.

In order to ensure that interested parties become paying advertisers, you have to ensure that your passive approach is set up to provide as much relevant information as possible. Your advertising link should include an option to request a media kit, which should include all of the relevant and updated analytics information along with a pricing plan for advertising. Having an updated media kit always ready for direct advertisers will increase your conversion rate and will ensure that you do not have to spend valuable time beating the bushes looking for advertisers.

Of course, you have to make advertising on your site worthwhile, so make sure that the information you provide is accurate and that you can deliver on any claims you make about your site and its audience. Having loyal advertisers is the best method to ensure consistent revenue from direct advertising, and recurring ads are a preferred method for maintaining a level of familiarity for returning visitors to the site.

Sponsored Content - Paid Advertorials

Sponsored content is quickly becoming one of the most preferred options among content marketing professionals, and this increasing demand is an exceptionally beneficial development for bloggers who understand precisely how to use advertorials correctly. While sponsored content is becoming increasingly popular, it remains something of a divisive issue among publishers who are concerned that this form of marketing will have an adverse impact on their brand. This is a valid concern that will be addressed in this chapter, as there are several ways that advertorials can be misleading when certain guidelines are not followed.

As a blogger who must be loyal to your audience, the decision to opt for sponsored content in the form of paid advertorials is a difficult one. If you have talked to other bloggers about the subject, you are probably well aware of the strong opinions that exist on the subject. This should not dissuade you from considering the use of this kind of content, especially if you are committed to transparency with your audience and are only willing to support sponsored content that accurately reflects your personal values and beliefs. Adopting a consistent and transparent approach while using this strategy can allow you to generate a significant amount of revenue while still remaining loyal to the audience that supports you.

A Preferred Option for Marketers

Shrewd marketing professionals know the value of utilizing

sponsored content, as some of the more traditional online options are not nearly as effective in generating the kind of results companies desire out of a marketing campaign. Savvy Internet users simply ignore banner ads and click away from pop-up advertising as quickly as they are able, and marketing research has demonstrated time and again that the best way to reach consumers is by utilizing a number of varied in-text strategies, including the use of advertorials.

The rapid growth of this strategy is directly tied to the consistent success it generates, but that does not mean marketers have had it easy when it comes to finding sites willing to host this kind of content. Publications worry that sponsored content will have a negative effect on editorial integrity, as though using sponsored content would compromise their neutrality and their trustworthiness in the eyes of their readers. If a publisher or a blogger uses an advertorial in a way that is misleading, then the perception among readers will absolutely be altered in a negative fashion. While this may be true, it is simply not the case that sponsored content has to be misleading by definition.

Avoiding Potential Drawbacks

There are clear concerns among all kinds of sites regarding the use of sponsored content, but most of these concerns are misplaced or unfounded. Only bloggers and publications that have misused sponsored content have opened themselves up to criticism, most often as a result of trying to pass off sponsored content as just another post or article. This strategy misleads readers in the worst way possible and should be avoided at all costs. Transparency is necessary for the successful use of advertorials, as failing to identify sponsored content is the surest way to quickly alienate your readership in a permanent way.

Blending Sponsored Content

There is a fine line between seamlessly blending sponsored content and purposefully misleading readers regarding the use of sponsored content. It is best to make sure you are on the right side of that fine line so that you do not unintentionally turn away your loyal readers, so make sure any advertorial appearing on the site is clearly labeled as such. Even though it might seem counterintuitive, most marketing analyses show that while readers click on these articles at a reduced rate, the ones who do open the article become engaged at the same rate as any other article appearing on the site.

The key is to make sure the sponsored article is engaging and includes a headline that attracts readers without misleading them. When I use this type of marketing, I always preface the headline with "Sponsored Content" followed by a colon and the headline. In the article itself, I make it abundantly clear in the opening paragraph that the article is sponsored by an outside company for the purpose of promoting their product or service. While everyone has different standards for how to maintain a level of editorial integrity in using an advertorial, I believe that abiding by a few simple guidelines will ensure that readers are not turned away when they see sponsored content on a site.

Maintaining Editorial Integrity

Transparency is not the only strategy necessary for maintaining your editorial integrity and keeping the trust of your readers. The sponsored content you allow on your site ought to reflect your values and beliefs because once you support a substandard product or service on your website, the trust of your audience will quickly erode. This is why I only allow advertorials for products and services that I believe are of interest to my audience and that I know are of the highest quality. I never want to feel like my word is for sale to the highest bidder, so I ask myself a very simple question each time I evaluate an advertorial opportunity: "Is this a post you would be willing to write even if you were not getting paid for it?"

If the answer to that question is "no" -- or even if the answer is "maybe" -- I won't take those advertising dollars. It is as simple as that, and since the successful use of sponsored content relies on sites that are highly relevant to the product or service, it is highly likely that you will be familiar with what is being marketed. If you are not familiar with the product or service, either pass on supporting it publicly or become familiar with the product or service by using it yourself. In the long run, an honest and thoughtful approach to sponsored content is also the most profitable one.

Display Advertising - Banners and Graphics

As one of the longest-running tools available to marketers, display advertising is yet another potential source of revenue for your blog. Of all the available advertising options, display advertising holds tremendous value to blog owners because of its dependability with regard to demand. While banners and graphics have been at the core of marketing campaigns for many years now, blog owners still have a variety of issues to consider when it comes to developing an overarching strategy for implementation.

The question with display advertising is not -- like many other forms of revenue-generating strategies -- whether or not you should use it, but rather how you should use it. Readers expect banner advertising on every page they visit, as most understand that blogs depend on advertising revenue in order to provide freely available content to readers. Even with the widespread availability of ad blockers, marketing professionals still understand the value of display advertising and recognize that blogs offer an opportunity to reach an important segment of the consumer population.

With this in mind, it is worth noting that there is a point in which display advertising becomes obtrusive, so you have to be cautious regarding the number of ads you include in order to maintain the quality of the site experience for the reader. In a similar vein, you have to be judicious in choosing which type of advertisements are featured on your site, as it is possible to alienate your core readership by featuring ads that are inappropriate or offensive. This chapter will detail

14

everything you need to know about display advertising, including how to properly implement banners on your site and how to set prices that maximize your blog's revenue potential.

A Proven Strategy

For marketers, display advertising represents a core strategy that has been proven effective time and again. Display advertising can utilize a number of features specifically designed to draw the attention of a target audience, including:

• Images
• Audio
• Video
• Rich media

These features help offset the issue of "banner blindness," which is a term used to describe the behavior of readers who are familiar with the layout of most websites and have become savvy enough to ignore banner ads in order to quickly get to the content without distraction. The response of the marketing industry has been to use certain features to attract the attention of even the savviest of users, relying on interactive ads along with ads that feature audio or video, many of which are set to automatically play as soon as the page loads.

The efficacy of these strategies is both a good thing and a bad thing for bloggers, as these types of ads ensure continued demand for their placement on websites but also create the possibility that certain types of ads may alienate readers in a manner that drives them away from the site altogether. It is for this reason that bloggers have to understand the importance of selectivity when it comes to adopting a display advertising strategy on their site.

Importance of Selectivity

As we have discussed in previous chapters, there is such a thing as too much advertising. A blog can become cluttered very quickly if too many ads are used or if they are placed in a way that becomes obtrusive to the reader. This aspect of display advertising is one of the few drawbacks, but that does not mean you should avoid display ads altogether, as it is fairly simple to adopt a few guidelines to help prevent any issues that may harm your site. The goal, after all, is to generate revenue without affecting the user experience.

Without visiting them, think about the sites you frequent and the advertising they use. Of those sites -- again, without visiting them -- try to identify how many ads are on the site, where they are placed and which kinds of ads are being used. Now go ahead and visit the site and see how accurately you were able to identify the advertising strategies. If these sites use more ads than you estimated, it is safe to say that the ads were placed in an unobtrusive way that did not affect your visitor experience. This is what you should be trying to cultivate through the use of selectivity: Ads that are seen by the reader but do not interfere with the reader's experience.

Determining Price Points

There are several ways that you can sell display advertising space on your website. We have already discussed direct sales and how to passively attract advertisers to your site, and there are other programs like Adsense that guarantee that your available ad space will be filled in exchange for a percent of the advertising revenue. Adsense and other programs similar to it will be discussed in a later chapter, so for now we will discuss how to determine the most effective pricing system for direct ad sales.

Ad placement is a key component of valuation, so it is essential that you have an understanding of where your readers focus the majority of their attention while on your site. This can be done through the use of heatmaps, which show where users tend to be most focused while on the site, providing a simple visualization of the ad spaces that are most valuable.

The size of the ad and the amount of traffic the site generates also play a role in determining the price of each ad, and I recommend using a very simple formula that is appropriate for identifying a price point guideline for the majority of sites: The number of site visitors per day divided by 10 equals the dollar amount you can charge per month for each display advertisement. For example, a site that gets 1,500 visitors per day could charge $150 per month for each banner ad they sell.

When used on its own, this formula does not properly leverage the potential value of the site, so some adjustments have to be made based on the placement of the advertisement and the site's core subject. A niche site, for example, may be able to charge twice as much for advertising if its readership is representative of a marketer's specific target audience. The same can be said with regard to ad placement, as some ad placements are simply more valuable than others. This formula is simply a solid guideline from which to start a comprehensive pricing plan for advertising.

Advertising Networks - Adsense on a Small Blog?

Adsense is a popular option among bloggers, and for good reason: It represents a simple way to generate revenue and requires little initial effort to get started. Most experienced bloggers have used Adsense at some point in time, and it should come as no surprise that there are some divisive views on whether or not it makes sense to utilize Adsense on a blog. Since the opinions on Adsense are so divided, this chapter will outline both sides of the issue, first taking a look at the positive aspects of the program before moving on to a discussion of some of the drawbacks.

The Good

With such widespread use on sites of all sizes, it should be plainly evident that Adsense is one of the most sought-after advertising programs available to publishers. Of the positive aspects of Adsense, most bloggers will cite each of the following benefits as a reason for opting to use the program:

• Little effort required to use Adsense
• Provides an immediate source of revenue
• Ad space is always filled
• Ads are always specifically targeted

These reasons all represent significant benefits related to the use of Adsense, and it is helpful to go over each one in greater detail so that you can make an informed decision on whether these benefits are consistent with your specific revenue goals.

Adsense Requires Little Effort

The Adsense program makes generating revenue fairly simple by using a system that is almost fully automated, allowing bloggers to focus on other aspects of running their blog without having to devote much time or energy to securing advertisers. As long as the blog meets some basic requirements of the program (contact information, privacy policy, etc.), the application process is simple and acceptance into the program is all but guaranteed. Once the blog is accepted, Adsense provides the owner with instructions for choosing the placement of ads on the site. Ads then appear immediately and remain filled for the duration of the Adsense agreement.

Creating an Immediate Revenue Stream

The site evaluation process takes about two weeks to a month, and ads can be placed on the site immediately following the approval of the site. Adsense then tracks the number of clicks the ads generate and the site owner receives a monthly check based on the volume and value of the clicks. This immediate source of revenue is appealing to bloggers for obvious reasons, as this represents one of the quickest ways to monetize a blog.

Ad Space Is Always Occupied

When you sell ads directly you have to make sure that all of your ad space is filled at all times. With Adsense, there is no concern that any ad space will go unused, as Adsense keeps these spaces continuously filled with no effort required on your part. This is extremely convenient and ensures that your site can rely on a consistent stream of revenue for as long as you remain a part of the program. This same level of consistent ad placement cannot be guaranteed through direct sales, though it should be noted that there are many useful and effective strategies for keeping ad space consistently filled if you choose to go with a direct sales route.

Ads Are Specifically Targeted to Your Readers

When visiting sites using Adsense, you will probably notice that the ads are based on your personal interests and are often based on sites you recently visited or feature products you recently viewed. This is because Google tracks your interests and determines which ads to show you based on the likelihood that those ads will be of interest to you. This ensures that the advertising on your site is more likely to generate clicks from readers and bring in revenue for your blog, which is something that is not necessarily so easily accomplished through direct advertising sales.

The Bad

Of course, the Adsense program has its drawbacks as well, and many of the aforementioned benefits have certain caveats that apply. The targeted ads, for example, may advertise a product that the user only recently purchased, making it a wasteful use of ad space. Some of the other drawbacks include:

• Reduced long-term value
• Lack of control over ads
• Unintentional affiliations
• Revenue depends on visitors leaving the site

These are not insignificant issues with the program, and any one of these issues may be more than enough to dissuade you from using the program at all.

Potentially Inefficient Over the Long-Term

Adsense brings in immediate revenue, but it also reduces your opportunities for long-term profitability. The program takes a significant percentage of your ad revenue in exchange for the convenience of the program, and an established blog with lots of traffic does not have to do much to attract advertisers willing to pay much more for space than what the Adsense program generates. While attracting advertisers may be difficult at first, the initial effort may be worth ensuring that you receive 100 percent of the advertising revenue your site generates.

Lack of Control Over Ads

The program allows you to have some level of control over the type of ads that appear, but there is no way to guarantee that an ad you would not have otherwise approved will show up on your site. It is hard to know what ads actually appear on the site because of the targeted approach used by Adsense, as the ads you see when you visit the site will be quite different than those that appear to someone who is in a different demographic or who has dissimilar interests. This can result in your site becoming unintentionally affiliated with a company or product you do not wish to support. Your readers won't know either, as many will assume that you are responsible for approving all of the content that appears on your site and will figure that every ad represents a tacit approval of a specific product or service.

Revenue Is Generated by Drawing Readers Away

Perhaps the most interesting aspect of the Adsense program is the fact that revenue is generated by luring readers away from the site. Many bloggers believe it is counterintuitive to use a program that requires clicks to generate revenue when those clicks lead a reader away from the site itself. While that may be true, Adsense supporters believe that their readers will return after clicking on an ad or will finish reading a blog post before moving on to check out an advertisement.

Affiliate Marketing - Amazon, ClickBank, Commission Junction

While many of the monetization strategies and programs we have thus far mentioned involve a fair amount of time committed to tasks other than writing and maintaining the blog, affiliate marketing represents one of the most efficient strategies for generating passive income. Bloggers who are part of one or more affiliate programs are able to earn commissions on the products or services they market through their blog, and this process can be highly lucrative when working with the right partner.

Choosing the right partner and adopting an honest approach to affiliate marketing is central to ensuring your blog is able to enjoy long-term profitability while maintaining a loyal readership. Even though SEO strategies are an essential part of promoting any blog, affiliate marketing programs often work best for blogs that have a recurring core audience that deeply trusts the blogger. Successful affiliate marketing is far more likely when your readers trust what you have to say and trust in the brand you are partnering with, so remember to exercise caution when choosing or promoting a brand.

An Overview of Affiliate Marketing

There are many different kinds of affiliate marketing programs available to bloggers. Each specific program operates in a different way, but they are all essentially based on the same premise: The affiliate receives a commission in exchange for promoting a certain brand's product or service. While this premise is the basis for just about every affiliate program, the commission rate, the method of promotion and brand's desired outcome can vary widely. For example, the brand may pay a commission based on three distinct outcomes:

• Purchases
• Registrations
• Visits

Each outcome requires different strategies on behalf of the affiliate, and certain outcomes may be more profitable for the blogger. If you, for example, ran a niche blog on avant-garde photography, an affiliate program that offered a commission on high-end camera equipment would be far more lucrative than a program with a commission based on referred visits. The former affiliate program would also allow you to promote products that you personally use and would legitimately be of interest to your readers, thereby ensuring that you can maintain the trust of your readers while also earning a commission.

To start out as an affiliate, bloggers do not often have to make any sort of investment or initial outlay to be part of a program. Most programs are completely commission-based, so there is no reason to be concerned over moving inventory or generating interest in a product that simply doesn't appeal to readers. It is for these reasons and more that affiliate marketing programs are viewed as one of the best passive income strategies available to bloggers, but that does not mean it is not a strategy that is without its drawbacks.

In some cases, affiliate marketing has been harmed by the presence of unscrupulous partners on both sides. Some affiliates have engaged in misleading practices for the sake of generating more sales with an eye on a greater commission, and some brands have lured affiliates by promising large commission rates only to drop them shortly thereafter. While it is regrettable that this occurs at all, the existence of those who lack scruples only underscores the importance of choosing an affiliate partner wisely. The commission rate should never be the sole determining factor, as your reputation will ultimately be tied to your brand partners.

As for specific affiliate programs, this chapter will offer an analysis of three of the more popular brands bloggers choose to work with:

• Amazon
• ClickBank
• Commission Junction

These programs have varying features that may make them appealing to one blogger but not to another. When you consider your options, it is essential to evaluate how each program suits your specific blogging needs. Your blog's core subject, your reader demographics and your personal goals should all play central roles in the decision-making process, so be sure to thoroughly analyze the benefits each individual program can provide.

Amazon

The appeal of Amazon's affiliate program should be clear: An established, trusted and immediately recognizable company that offers a diverse array of products on its site. The expansive product offerings mean that just about any blog could employ the affiliate program while only promoting products that are highly relevant to its core subject matter. Since there are so many products available for promotion, repeat visitors to the site will see different products that may be of legitimate interest, helping to secure a constant stream of passive income.

The most frequently cited drawback to the program is the relatively low commission rate. The rate is frequently less than 10 percent, but the sheer magnitude of the product offerings ensures that bloggers are able to choose highly specific products that are more likely to be purchased by readers. The fact that the product is offered by Amazon and not a lesser-known retailer will also increase the likelihood of purchases, so the low commission rates are frequently offset by the volume of sales.

ClickBank

ClinkBank affiliates enjoy large commissions from a broad base of products, which is why it remains one of the more popular options among bloggers. Many bloggers prefer ClinkBank because of the security the program offers due to its status as the retailer. Some unscrupulous vendors in other programs will attempt to bypass the commission by engaging in deceitful practices like pretending the buyer ultimately returned the product. This cannot happen with ClinkBank, as vendors who attempt to do this will lose their sale as well, creating a disincentive to engage in this practice.

Commission Junction

Commission Junction's program operates in much the same way as other affiliate programs, as it is simple to navigate the signup process and enables bloggers to have access to some of the most highly sought-after products to promote. This program in particular may appeal to niche bloggers -- especially those who operate several different niche sites -- as the products are searchable according to some very specific terms. This affiliate program is serious about seeing its bloggers succeed, so make sure your blog is ready to be monetized -- accounts that have gone six months without generating a commissionable transaction are automatically dropped from the program.

Branded Sponsored Campaigns - Ford, Nutella, Albertsons, Disney and More!

When you have built up a large enough following, PR specialists will begin to seek your assistance in reaching a wider audience. This is especially the case if your blog is focused on a subject that draws a readership coinciding with a brand's target audience. As a result, branded sponsored campaigns from major companies such as Ford, Nutella, Albertsons and Disney represent excellent opportunities to generate income for your blog.

Branded sponsorship campaigns are not just a one-time opportunity. If you are able to drive conversions for the company and can clearly demonstrate your blog's value to the brand, then you will see an abundance of future opportunities as well. As established brands with big marketing budgets, these companies are in a unique position to offer bloggers a sense of security that is hard to match. When a branded sponsorship opportunity presents itself, you have to be ready to quickly evaluate the benefits of doing so and come up with a piece of native advertising that meets each of the following requirements:

- Relevant
- Targeted
- Credible

When sponsored content in the form of native advertising appears on your blog, you ought to make sure that you are considering the needs of the brand along with the needs of your readers. As with other forms of sponsored content, always maintain transparency and endeavor to offer an honest and personal account that is relevant to the brand.

The Importance of Relevance

Understanding how to effectively write a piece for a branded sponsored campaign is incredibly important. When writing one of these pieces, you should recognize the importance of relevance as it relates to the campaign, your audience and your personal expertise. For readers to continue to trust you and the brand you are writing about, the subject you address must be one that you and the brand are qualified to discuss as experts.

Ford, for example, may wish to reach a more technologically-inclined audience by commissioning a tech blogger to write a post on Ford's efforts to move automotive technology forward. The blogger could ensure relevance to both the site and the company by writing about Ford's practical approach to autonomous cars, including the patient-but-steady implementation of autonomous driving systems as a means of transitioning to a future in which it appears increasingly likely to be dominated by fully automated vehicles. The subject is relevant to all of the parties involved and accomplishes Ford's campaign goal of demonstrating its commitment to advancing automotive technology.

Identifying a Target Audience

While identifying a target audience is one of the prime

responsibilities of the advertising campaign manager, it is also a responsibility that bloggers would benefit from adopting as well. A branded sponsored campaign surely targets members of your audience, but it is your task to create content that appeals to your audience in a way that clearly benefits the brand. Your job is to entertain and inform by writing the native advertising in a way that shows your readers that the brand provides products and services that are beneficial in a variety of ways that specifically apply to them. Since these are your audience members, you should already understand how to adopt a targeted approach that appeals to their specific interests so that the sponsored content campaign is able to accomplish its goal.

Product Placement

There should be an obvious reason why a brand wants to place native advertising on your site, and the content you create should employ the same voice and style you use in every other piece you post. This means that there should be a somewhat seamless incorporation of the sponsored content within your site, though it is important to again note that you should always be transparent about the fact that the content is sponsored.

This applies to the topic and the way it is approached as well. If you typically post restaurant reviews that focus on chefs who push the boundaries of culinary innovation, then it makes little sense to post a step-by-step recipe that incorporates Nutella in some way. It would make more sense to instead craft a review of a restaurant with a chef that actually includes menu offerings featuring Nutella. Maintaining the continuity of the site benefits your site as a whole and also increases the effectiveness of the branded sponsored campaign.

Maintaining Credibility

There is nothing wrong with using your blog to generate income even if it means accepting payment to write about a specific brand or topic as a part of a marketing campaign. As long as readers do not feel as though they are being misled they will continue to frequent your site and will continue to trust what you have to say. In order to accomplish this, however, you may have to turn down some opportunities to participate in a branded sponsored campaign. After all, losing your credibility with your audience will also mean that you will lose future opportunities to write sponsored content, so do not feel obligated to accept every offer and always be honest when you feel conflicted about a specific brand, product or subject.

How Ford, Nutella, Albertsons and Disney Effectively Use Native Advertising

It should come as little surprise that some of the largest corporations have developed a successful approach when it comes to one of the fastest-growing marketing strategies. These companies have had their sponsored content featured in highly respected publications like The New York Times and The Atlantic, both of which have high editorial standards and, of course, clearly label that the piece is sponsored by a specific brand.

These brands not only target the massive audiences of these publications, as there is clearly value in working with a blog that has a smaller audience with specific and relevant interests -- especially when that audience feels a sense of loyalty to the specific blogger. The fact that these pieces are transparent in identifying their status as sponsored content ensures that publishers maintain their integrity while brands are able to reach its target audience in a way that is both entertaining and informative.

Build a Mailing List - How to Sell to Your Subscribers

It is shocking how few bloggers take full advantage of the benefits inherent in a strong mailing list, particularly when one considers just how lucrative a mailing list can be when built properly and used in the right way. There are countless bloggers whose main source of revenue comes directly from their mailing list, and that does not include the indirect benefits that accompany a well-built mailing list.

Perhaps the idea of a mailing list is unappealing because you are all too familiar with mailing lists that only succeed in cluttering your inbox every day before getting deleted. It is certainly the case that some bloggers make improper use of their mailing lists to the point in which it ceases to be beneficial, but that does not mean it is not entirely worthwhile to learn the practices and strategies that lead to a mailing list being useful to both the subscriber and the blogger alike.

An Overlooked Approach

Every blogger should have a mailing list through which they can make announcements and provide updates that are likely to interest their readers. It is an incredibly convenient way to reach a large group of people without very little effort, yet many bloggers do not realize just how central a mailing list should be when it comes to their overarching strategy.

A mailing list drives traffic to the site, improves brand recognition, increases audience loyalty and provides publishers with another means through which they can generate revenue. Why it remains an overlooked approach is something of a mystery, so this chapter will outline the specific reasons for developing a mailing list and will demonstrate the best methods for building and managing the list properly.

Extremely Valuable to Advertisers

Advertisers, perhaps more so than many bloggers, recognize the value of a strong mailing list and are quick to purchase ad space on a newsletter they know will be seen by a broad audience. This is because these ads are more effective when it comes to achieving a desired outcome, making them far more valuable to a blogger. Since mailing list ads are separate from the site itself, this represents additional ad space that brings in more revenue without cluttering the site or its design. It is hard to make sense of the fact that more bloggers are not building a mailing list when it creates additional advertising space that is far more valuable and would not even exist otherwise.

Building the Mailing List

Building a mailing list is far from complicated, and there are really only two things you need to build a strong list in short order:

• Outstanding content
• Clear calls to action

It should be obvious that no one is going to want to sign up for a mailing list that does not consistently offer something of clear value to the reader. People who sign up for a mailing list only do so for one of two reasons: They were either tricked into signing up or they value what they have read so much that they do not want to miss another post. Clearly the latter strategy is the only one that results in long-term subscribers, so you have to make sure that your blog posts are consistently informative and inherently valuable to readers.

The second aspect of building a list requires you to be a bit more creative and even a bit aggressive. A call to action is your final sales pitch, and it should be far more than a passive or polite request to sign up for your mailing list. Your call to action should clearly explain why it is beneficial to join the mailing list and should make it easy for interested parties to do so with little effort at all. When you have consistently outstanding content and you aggressively market your mailing list, you are bound to be more likely to have a mailing list that continues to grow over time.

Employing Strategies to Ensure Growth and Retention

Nobody likes being tricked into joining a mailing list, yet many companies still automatically subscribe customers after a purchase or use some other disingenuous tactic to bulk up their mailing list. These strategies work in building a list, but they are hardly effective when it comes to improving loyalty among readers or creating a list that generates the kind of results you are looking for. Instead, a list that has 100,000 subscribers will be read by only a small percentage and deleted by the rest. A mailing list only has value if its recipients actually read the content it includes and return to the site over and over again.

You can ensure that your mailing list continues to grow and that you retain your existing subscribers by being judicious with your use of the list. Do not waste the time of your subscribers by sending out information unless you know it has clear value and will be appreciated by your readers. Only use the mailing list when it is necessary to do so, as your readers will recognize that you value their time and only use your mailing list when you believe it is beneficial to the reader. This level of respect will help your list grow and will ensure that readers do not unsubscribe, which makes your list exponentially more valuable to advertisers.

Leveraging the Value of the List

The real benefit of the mailing list is the many different ways you can use it to generate revenue. The mailing list can be used to promote new posts or to inform readers of the new products and services you may be offering, or you can generate revenue from other bloggers who are looking to build a strong mailing list of their own. You just have to make sure you do not overuse your list to the point where its effectiveness is limited, so remember to be judicious and only leverage the strength of your list when there is a clear benefit to the subscriber in doing so.

www.ingramcontent.com/pod-product-compliance
Lightning Source LLC
Chambersburg PA
CBHW051218050326
40689CB00008B/1353